Retired

Other titles in the *Crikey I'm*... series

Crikey I'm A Teenager

Crikey I'm Thirty

Crikey I'm Forty

Crikey I'm Fifty

Crikey I'm In Love

Crikey I'm Getting Married

Crikey I'm A Mum

Crikey I'm A Dad

Crikey I'm A Grandparent

Crikey I'm...™
Retired

Contributors

Dr David Haslam
Victoria Warner
Eliza Williams

Edited by

Steve Hare

Cover Illustration by

Ian Pollock

PURPLE HOUSE

Published by Purple House Limited 1998
75 Banbury Road
Oxford OX2 6PE

© Purple House Limited 1998

Cover illustrations: © Ian Pollock/The Inkshed

Crikey I'm... is a trademark of Purple House
Limited

A catalogue record for this book is available
from the British Library

ISBN 1-84118-015-7

Printed in Great Britain by
Cox and Wyman

Acknowledgements

We are grateful to everyone who helped in the compilation of this book, particularly to the following:

Stephen Franks of Franks and Franks (Design)

Inform Group Worldwide (Reproduction)

Dave Kent of the Kobal Collection

Office of National Statistics

Bodleian Library, Oxford

Central Library, Oxford

British Film Institute

Liz Brown

Mark McClintock

Hannah Wren

Illustrations

Contents

Crikey, I'm Retired!

So – the day has come at last. We shall not say 'the great day', at least not without a certain degree of qualification. Retirement is approached by many with trepidation; some dread it. It's an enormous change in your way of life, and probably your income, too.

It is quite possible that you are appalled at the thought of having nothing to do, no reason to get up early in the morning, no need to live life at that unnaturally frantic pace, racing to catch trains, fuming in traffic jams, meeting endless deadlines. It is as if there were no longer any purpose to life.

On the other hand, there are all those chores and jobs you always promised you would get around to. There are friends you have neglected, distant relations you simply never had time to visit. You suddenly have a unique opportunity to put your life in order: to rearrange your schedules and adjust your pace to something a little more seemly, perhaps, but a whole lot more natural. You are unlikely to miss the stress.

Retirement offers a unique opportunity to think about *yourself* for a change. Just stop and wonder for a moment. Leaving aside those occasional treats and all too brief holidays, your entire life, from the onset of adulthood, has been devoted to others.

For the most part this is not anything you might begrudge. Bringing up children demands constant sacrifice: you happily devoted yourselves to such a task. Then there was work. Even the self-employed can hardly say they were working for themselves. The customer always came first. You could not even relax on holiday – the phone might be ringing at home with a lucrative job you just missed. For the rest, there was the rat-race. A daily commute which degenerated over the years into a stressful grind. Your entire working life was devoted to the company – probably several companies, these days. But your life was never your own.

Now it is. The trouble is, in many cases, all that means is you are now going to devote yourself to countless causes, charities and good deeds. That's great!

But spare a little time for you, and yours.

Past Masters

A Brief History of Retirement

In the last few years a lot of thought has gone into redefining the terms we use to describe the approach and state of retirement. It is not so very long ago that people retiring at 60 or 65 would receive their 'old age pension', and be known as OAPs. It's a tricky business: one might even say a grey area. The terms 'third age', 'golden years', even 'retired' all lack something. As a compromise, 'senior citizen' still takes some beating. The term implies that the person is

In 2026, 28.3% of the total UK population will be aged 60 or over.

still actively involved in society and still has a valuable contribution to make. Being a citizen implies certain rights and duties. Being senior implies that a degree of deference and respect is due.

Ancient societies revered the elders in their society. Merely surviving to a considerable age was an achievement. But along the way they became a repository of knowledge about the history and traditions of the tribe, as well as the practical matters of raising children, livestock and crops. Their age and experience gave them the right to pass judgement. Their memories and knowledge

The government is proposing to equalise the state pension age at 65 for men and women – although not until 2010.

Henry Wilcoxon takes it easy in *The President's Mystery*, 1936.

passed on to their children and grandchildren forged vital links between the past and future.

The United States of America, home of political correctness and the terror of treading on anyone's toes, can be relied upon to have given more thought than is absolutely necessary to the ticklish subject of nomenclature, and to have come up with a whole raft of expressions and organisations, including the radical age-conscious organisation, the Gray Panthers. Nevertheless, it is also in the United States that the *Crone Chronicles* are published.

But while terminology is keeping up with the times, legislation and attitudes amongst government and employers still remain locked in a previous age. The simple fact is that at 60 or 65 these days, the average person is not worn out and exhausted, but closer to their prime of life. They may well deserve a break, but it should be a matter of individual choice rather than an obligation.

> **'When I was young, the Dead Sea was still alive.'**
>
> George Burns

At the start of the twentieth century only a small proportion of the population – around five per cent – were expected to survive

> **65 year-olds spend an average of £1.70 on the National Lottery per week.**

PROJECT FUND

2025 Pennsylvania Ave., NW, Suite 821
Washington, DC 20006

America's retired population take positive action against age discrimination.

THE UNIVERSITY OF THE THIRD AGE

The U3A offers a unique opportunity for study later in life.

beyond 65. Retirement, after more than 50 years' hard manual labour, often outdoors or in unregulated factory conditions, made sense.

Since that time, there has been a more or less constant improvement in diet, general health and working conditions. The nature of the workplace has changed radically, with agricultural and heavy industry giving way to office employment and skilled labour. Hours of work have gradually reduced, and annual paid leave has increased. Those approaching retirement find themselves often feeling cheated by outmoded legislation, and living in fear from their mid forties onwards because narrow-minded employers have taken the view that anyone over 30 is not worthy of consideration as a potential new employee.

This attitude is slowly being overcome, as organisations begin to cotton on to the fact that a mature, responsible and experienced employee has considerably more to offer, and not just in terms of loyalty and dependability. More and more people, forced by company policy into what is essentially premature retirement, are finding gainful employment as consultants to their previous employers. Many more have set up their own small businesses in the fields they know best.

In 1994, less than 51% of men aged 60–64 were in paid jobs; 69% of women aged 55–59 worked.

Retirement, then, may simply mean a change in the terms and conditions of your employment, rather than a full-stop to a career in mid-flow.

All the same, the prospect of retirement is not something to be shut away in a drawer like an insurance policy document. Today's school-leavers and graduates are being encouraged to think about their retirement and start planning their finances. The simple mathematics of population trends demands it.

In comparison to the five per cent of people at pensionable age at the beginning of the century, that figure is already approaching 20 per cent.

A Little Respect

In Japan, there is – in September – a national 'Respect for the Aged' day.

A man at 60 today can expect to live another 18 years on average, almost a quarter of his lifespan; a woman can expect 22 years. The French refer to this 'third age' as the 'age of living'. It's a time to travel, to take up study once more, perhaps through the University of the Third Age. It is a time to pursue interests, to visit friends and family, to contribute to society through various organisations and charities, serving on local or parish councils, or taking up duties as a magistrate. Alternatively you might just want to get your garden right, or take advantage of travel concessions to visit other gardens. In other words, retirement offers virtually limitless opportunities. More and more, it is regarded as a new beginning, to be welcomed and lived to the full.

Ten Films You Finally Have Time To Watch

1. *The Great Escape* (173 minutes)

2. *The Godfather* (175 minutes)

3. *Dances With Wolves* (180 minutes)

4. *JFK* (189 minutes)

5. *Titanic* (195 minutes)

6. *Spartacus* (196 minutes)

7. *Ben-Hur* (217 minutes)

8. *Gone With The Wind* (220 minutes)

9. *The Ten Commandments* (220 minutes)

10. *Napoleon* (378 minutes)

Time to spare . . .
with _this_ power mower

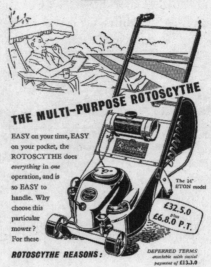

THE MULTI-PURPOSE ROTOSCYTHE

EASY on your time, EASY on your pocket, the ROTOSCYTHE does _everything_ in one operation, and is so EASY to handle. Why choose this particular mower? For these

The 14" ETON model

£32.5.0
plus
£6.8.0 P.T.

ROTOSCYTHE REASONS :

DEFERRED TERMS
available with initial
payment of £13.3.0

- Light and easy to handle, the _engine_ does the cutting.
- Cuts any length of grass by unique rotary action — your "after holidays" and "bad weather" troubles removed.
- Slices through all stalks, leaving a perfect finish.
- Collects _all_ grass by vacuum suction.
- A full year's guarantee.

- Sucks up leaves, stalks, pine needles, etc., no raking.
- It even removes moss by a simple adjustment.
- Gives an immaculate, smooth, banded finish.
- No regrinding, saving pounds each year.
- A free demonstration can be arranged.

For full details of the improved ETON model,
and other Rotoscythes, together with the name of
your nearest agent, write to

Rotoscythe target the retired generation in 1955.

10

How It Worked Out

Changes in the Workplace

Most people retiring now started work in the 1950s, when times were very different. It was a time of austerity and prosperity mixed: at the very beginning of the decade, rationing was still in force, and times were hard for many – particularly following the dramatic devaluation of the pound in 1949. By 1957, however, Harold Macmillan was announcing that 'you've never had it so good', and the economy started to boom. During the same year, virtual full employment was achieved, whilst the annual rate of growth of the gross national product was an unprecedented 2.6 per cent.

Who Was Working

1957: marked effectively full employment.

1966: 437,229 were unemployed.

1972: unemployment reaches 1 million for the first time.

1980: unemployment stands at 2 million.

1987: unemployment hovers just below 3 million.

1998: the unemployment figure was 1.86 million.

The sixties continued the trend towards prosperity and general economic growth. In 1961, Britain formally applied for EEC entry; when the country finally joined in 1973, the economy again changed dramatically. At about this time many people acquired a car, as purchase tax was cut, leading to an accelerated consumer boom. Unemployment was still low, so the chances of being in continual work were very good: wages, however, were subject to occasional 'freezing' by the government, who were continually worried about the rate of inflation and wage increases.

> **'I'm at an age where my back goes out more than I do.'**
> Phyllis Diller

During the seventies the working environments of many people changed beyond all recognition. From the very beginning of the decade it was clear that this was to be the era of the strike, when British troops were ordered on standby to keep the ports open during a national dockers' walkout. Shortly after that, it was

> **In 1994, there were 10.6 million people of a pensionable age in Great Britain, representing 18.2% of the total population.**

announced that strikes were at their highest since 1926: no less than 8.8 million working days had been lost by November of 1970. It was into this era that decimal currency was born: suddenly the wage packet no longer contained shillings or old pence.

The strikes continued in 1972. A shortage of coal led directly to the imposition of the three-day week, when many people found themselves with much time on their hands, and very little coal in their bunkers.

Domestic bliss during the retirement years!

"HOW CAN MY SAVINGS KEEP UP WITH THE COST OF LIVING?"

Buy Retirement Issue National Savings Certificates and help protect the buying power of your savings.

They're linked to the General Index of Retail Prices (R.P.I.), a sort of 'shopping basket' which records the movement of prices from month to month.

e.g. If you hold £100 worth of certificates and the R.P.I. goes up 12% during the period since purchase, you get back £112, providing the certificates have been held at least one year.

Plus a 4% bonus on your original investment if you hold your certificates for 5 years.

Free of all UK income tax and capital gains tax.

If you should ever need to cash in your certificates in a hurry, it only takes a matter of days. And as long as you've held them for over one year, they're index-linked in the normal way.

Retirement Certificates are sold in £10 units. Maximum holding is £500 which may be held in addition to holdings of any other issues of National Savings Certificates.

Ask for a leaflet at your Post Office or Trustee Savings Bank.

INDEX LINKED

National Savings Certificates Retirement Issue

Advice to the retired from National Savings in 1970.

The three-day week made a return appearance for several months in 1973, with Anthony Barber's 'crisis budget' which cut public spending dramatically, and constricted industry to three days of electricity consumption per week. Things remained bleak throughout the mid-seventies; in 1975 the biggest monthly increase in unemployment since the Second World War was recorded. The pound sank, and the number of striking workers continued to rise as more unions pushed forward higher wage claims.

The next major upheaval, of course, was in 1979 when the Tories and Margaret Thatcher won the general election. Within a matter of months MPs approved her bid to sell off nationalised industries, and once again the face of Britain's economy was set for spectacular change. Thatcher's debut as Prime Minister was appropriately marked by British Steel who, in 1980, axed 11,287 jobs in Wales. Unemployment stood at 1.89 million, and with new redundancies totalling 40,000 a month, it was clear that Britain was sliding inexorably into depression.

> ### *What They Earned*
>
> In **1950** the average weekly wage was **£5.75**.
> In **1997** the average weekly wage was **£289**.

Sure enough, during 1981 unemployment topped 2.5 million, and riots broke out across many of the major cities and towns in England. Community leaders blamed racist policing methods, together with unemployment; and the poor standard of housing.

In 1983 the wage packet changed once again, when the £1 coin came into circulation. Ironically, at this point the pound itself was particularly weak and the economy generally was still rather precarious. The miners' strike in 1984 increased hardships for many miners' families, and was to do so for the next year.

Meanwhile, in the City, the Yuppies ('young, upwardly-mobile people') were taking over. The economy picked up, and was followed by a dramatic boom in prosperity: initiative and ambition were the key words in an acquisitive society. The Stock Exchange dealer's life was revolutionised by computers and other innovations; whilst every office had to be complete with computer, fax and the latest in business technology. The Yuppies found mobile phones, sharp suits and Filofaxes to be indispensable. If you were house-buying at this point, it was something of a seller's market: house prices in London were rising at £1,000 per month in 1987.

Such a boom couldn't last. The Black Monday crash in October 1987 wiped £50 billion off the value of companies on the London Stock Exchange, and marked the official start of a recession that was to bite hard right up until the early nineties.

Interior Hall, Weald Regnis, Kennent

$\mathscr{L}$EADERSHIP

ROBERT ADAM was the first to design a house, its decoration
and furniture as a whole. After 200 years, his originals — and others influenced
by them — are superlative examples of gracious living.

Ford of Dagenham have achieved a similar unity in car design. Ford performance and
comfort are combined with a gracious beauty
of line and detail — and at a low cost.

Ford MOTORING
IS 'FIVE-STAR' MOTORING
THE BEST AT LOWEST COST
★ ★ ★ ★ ★

FORD MOTOR COMPANY LIMITED · DAGENHAM

Did you drive this car to work in 1953?

Things, then, are very different now. Relatively high levels of unemployment are taken for granted; jobs are taken on a short-term basis, and are no longer for life. On a brighter note, however, working conditions are better for most people than they have ever been; discrimination is gradually being eradicated; and opportunities for promotion and success are now (at least theoretically) equally available for both male and female, black and white, able-bodied or handicapped.

What They Drove

In 1955 there were	3.5 million cars
	14 people per car
In 1973 there were	13.5 million cars
	4 people per car
In 1997 there were	23 million cars
	2.5 people per car

In 1997, life expectancy at birth in Britain was 74 years for men, and nearly 80 years for women.
In Australia, it is 75 for men and 81 for women.
In Hong Kong it is 76 for men and 82 for women.
In Japan it is 76 for men and 83 for women.

Women On Top

The Changing Role of Women at Work

Back in the 1950s, women counted for just 30 per cent of the total workforce, and only 1.5 million of these women were actually married. By contrast, in 1997, over eight million married women worked. The number of working women actually dropped during the early fifties, as demobbed soldiers reclaimed their jobs, and women were (often reluctantly) reinstated into the kitchen.

The Working Woman

In **1951**, women in work numbered 7 million and constituted 30% of the workforce.
In **1998**, women in work numbered 12 million and constituted 45% of the workforce.

Throughout the fifties, however, women were pushing for more rights and more responsibilities. Early on, in 1952, the House of Commons gave all-party support to the principle of equal pay for women: but it would be 1970 before the Bill reached its second reading; and 1976 before it actually came into effect. Even then, the Bill could hardly be called 'successful': at the end of the nineties, over 45 years since the issue was first raised, statistics have shown that in three-quarters of couples a woman earns at least 10 per cent less than her male partner.

Although the days of matching salaries are yet to come, there is no doubt that the whole balance of power in the workplace has changed during the

> **'The age of a woman doesn't mean a thing. The best tunes are played on the oldest fiddles.'**
>
> Sigmund Z. Engel

working lifetime of today's retired person: you have paved the way for a whole new generation of men and women. Traditional bastions of male power have crumbled: in 1969, Lloyds of London admitted women through its doors for the very first time, and in 1973 female dealers were finally allowed on to the floor of the Stock Exchange.

Finally, of course, women now occupy more positions of power than ever before. For this we have to thank, at least partly, such successful public figures as Barbara Castle and Anita Roddick.

> **Men aged 65 consume an average of 11 units of alcohol per week. Women aged 65 consume 3 units per week.**

Throughout the eighties more and more women started to assume executive positions, as the idea of the female managing director became less of a dream and more of a reality. The reviews, over the last 20 years, of parental leave regulations, and the action taken against sex discrimination, have ensured that the future of women in industry is looking brighter than it ever has before.

The launch of *Yours* magazine, aimed specifically at the retired community, in 1974.

Sound advice from Prudential in 1952.

What Happened When

A Brief Review of the Last Fifty Years

It's been a sometimes traumatic, often dramatic, and generally eventful 50 years. Here is a list of just some events that have taken place during your working life.

1945
- Over 17,000 UK dockers strike over pay for a month.
- The IMF world bank is established.
- Press censorship in the UK ends.

1946
- The Royal Commission gives its stamp of approval to equal pay for women.
- IBM introduces the first electronic calculator.

1947
- Government bans mid-week sport in an attempt to boost work productivity.
- The Church warns against sexual temptation for young people in the workplace.
- BUPA is founded.

1948
- The NHS is formally introduced into the UK.
- The transistor is introduced into the world of technology.
- The rate of births is increasing dramatically, owing to couples' desire to 'catch up' on the lost war years.

1949

- The first jet airliner makes its maiden flight at 500mph.
- RCA announce a new system for broadcasting colour television.
- Britain's first launderette opens for a six-month trial in Bayswater.

1950s

1950

- The first J. Sainsbury's self-service store opens in Croydon.
- Frank Sinatra has a sell-out debut concert at the London Palladium.
- The bowler hat celebrates its centenary.

1951

- Aneurin 'Nye' Bevan and Harold Wilson resign from the Labour cabinet over proposed NHS charges for dental and optical services.
- Britain tests its first atomic bomb in the Indian Ocean.

1952

- King George VI dies in his sleep; two days later, Princess Elizabeth is pronounced Queen.
- The House of Commons votes for equal pay for women.
- London's last tram runs from Woolwich to New Cross.

1953

- Queen Elizabeth's coronation becomes the first to be seen live on television.

1954

- IBM invent a 'calculating electronic brain' available to rent at $25,000 a month.
- Rationing officially ends.
- Kidbrooke School, London's first comprehensive, is opened.

1955

- Churchill resigns as Prime Minister, and is replaced by Sir Anthony Eden.
- 16 Teddy Boys are arrested after a disturbance at Bath's dance-hall.

1956

- The film *Rock Around the Clock* causes riots when shown in British cinemas.

1957

- The European Common Market is set up.
- Eden resigns as Prime Minister and is replaced by Harold Macmillan.
- Benidorm in Spain becomes the new, as yet unspoilt holiday spot.

1958

- Race riots break out in Notting Hill.
- Prince Charles is created Prince of Wales by the Queen.
- Midland Bank is the first to introduce personal loans.

1959

- The first postcodes are inaugurated.

- Duty-free alcohol is available in airports in Preston and Renfrew.
- The Mini is first introduced.
- The M1 motorway is opened.

1960s

1960

- 344 tickets are issued on the first day of parking tickets and traffic wardens.
- Britain's first moving pavement, or 'Travelator' opens at Bank tube station.
- Stirling Moss is banned from driving for a year, after being found guilty of dangerous driving.

1961

- A Russian cosmonaut, Yuri Gagarin, is successfully launched into space.
- The contraceptive pill goes on sale in the UK.

1962

- 200 million viewers in 16 countries watch US television programmes by satellite for the first time.
- British weather reports start to give temperatures in centigrade, as well as in fahrenheit.

1963

- John Profumo offers to resign over rumours regarding an affair with Christine Keeler, but denies any impropriety; he resigns three months later, after admitting to lying.

The 'I'm Backing Britain' campaign begins in 1968; people are asked to work for half an hour for free in order to make Britain great once more.

1964

- Labour comes into power, with Harold Wilson as Prime Minister.
- BBC2 goes on air; its first programme is *Play School*.

1965

- Fighting continues between mods and rockers at seaside resorts.
- Cigarette advertisements are banned from television.
- The Beatles receive their MBEs.

1966

- London is officially 'swinging', particularly King's Road, Kensington Church Street, and Carnaby Street.
- Barclays Bank introduce the Barclaycard, the first British credit card.

1967

- It is the 'summer of love': flower power is 'in', and Twiggy popularises the 'waif' look.
- Barclays Bank introduce Britain's first cash dispensing machines.

1968

- First decimal coins come into circulation in Britain.
- The Beatles' Apple boutique in the West End opens.

1969

- Half a million people attend the three day Woodstock festival in the US.
- A new coin, the 50 pence piece, comes into circulation.

1970

- Strikes by dockers, national newspapers and local authorities in Britain throughout the year.
- The age of majority is reduced from 21 to 18.

1971

- Decimal currency is officially introduced into Britain.
- The Open University is launched, using television and radio amongst other teaching media.

1972

- Britain officially joins the EEC.
- The miners' strike causes blackouts for 20 days.

1973

- Measures are unveiled by the government intending to give women equality within the workplace.
- VAT is introduced.

1974

- Inflation in the UK soars to 16%, following VAT on petrol and the dropping of price control for nationalised industries.
- A government White Paper plans to outlaw sexual discrimination.

1975

- Margaret Thatcher becomes the leader of the Tory party in opposition.
- Unemployment levels reach over one million.

GOING METRIC-IN THE SHOPS

HOW TO TAKE IT EASY

Going metric is easier in practice than it sometimes sounds. All it really means is that you will be coming across more and more things being sold in metric quantities: metres for lengths, litres for liquids, and kilograms for weights. Some well-known things have gone metric recently and they may have caught your eye. Fabrics, for instance, are now sold by the metre; liquids like cooking oils and soft drinks in litres. Cornflakes now come in ½ kilogram packs, and from the middle of the year sugar will be in the shops in kilogram bags. It's quite probable that you have bought some of these things in metric already.

Here are some facts about metric weights and measures, and some simple rhymes which may help you remember comparisons between the new and the old.

WHY NOT CUT THIS OUT AND KEEP IT? ✂

metres

A metre measures three foot three
It's longer than a yard, you see

A metre (m) is approximately 3 inches longer than a yard

litres

A litre of water's
A pint and three quarters

A litre (*l*) is approximately 1¾ pints

kilograms

Two and a quarter pounds of jam
Weigh about a kilogram

A kilogram (kg) is approximately 2¼ lb

The Metrication Board 22 Kingsway, London WC2B 6LE

Guidance for the confused from the Metrication Board in 1976.

1976

• Harold Wilson resigns unexpectedly as Prime Minister, claiming to be physically and mentally exhausted.

• A prolonged heatwave in Britain causes widespread drought.

1977

• The British government abandons its 'social contract' with trade unions, following huge pay increase demands: national strikes continue.

• Seven IRA bombs explode in London's West End; the violence continues all year.

1978

• Anna Ford starts work as ITN's first woman newscaster.

• The BBC starts broadcasting permanently from the House of Commons.

1979

• Margaret Thatcher becomes Prime Minister; she announces plans for lower taxes and public spending, and later declares £3,500 million spending cuts, and increased prescription charges.

1980s

1980

• Margaret Thatcher announces that state benefit to strikers will be halved.

• Prince Charles marries Lady Diana Spencer.

1981

• The 'Gang of Four' (Roy Jenkins, Shirley Williams, David Owen and William Rodgers) break away from the Labour Party to form the new Social Democratic Party.

1982

• Channel 4 goes on air; a month later, concerns about bad language, political bias and over-emphasis on homosexuality and feminism are aired by critics.

1983

• The NHS is forced to privatise cleaning, catering and laundering services in a bid to save money.
• Cecil Parkinson resigns from the cabinet after having a relationship, and a child, with his secretary Sarah Keays.
• The pound coin comes into circulation.

1984

• A national miners' strike begins, after low pay increases and the beginning of pit closures; it continues until October, when many people return to work.

1985

• Bernie Grant is elected as the first black council leader; Wilfred Wood becomes the first black bishop.
• The Live Aid concert for Africa takes place at Wembley; the Live Aid appeal raises £50 million pounds.

1986

• The government launches a 'safe sex' campaign against AIDS, costing £20 million.

Retired and gardening in the fifties with Neverbend spades and forks (1955).

1987

- The Guinness scandal over insider dealing leads to the sacking and arrest of Ernest Saunders.
- 'Black Monday': the stock market crash causes the market to fall by 10 per cent.
- The Church gives the go-ahead for the ordination of women priests.

1988

- Margaret Thatcher becomes Britain's longest-serving Prime Minister this century.
- Nurses march to Parliament in support of pay claims and more money for the NHS, following Thatcher's plans to overhaul the system.

1989

- The European Community declares a ban on chlorofluorocarbons (CFCs).
- 94 football fans die at Liverpool's Hillsborough stadium, after too many fans are admitted to the ground.

1990s

1990

- Demonstrations against the Poll Tax are staged across Britain.
- Margaret Thatcher resigns and is replaced by John Major.
- The Commons Agriculture Committee says that there is no evidence to connect eating beef contaminated with BSE with a threat to human health.

1991

• The Birmingham Six are freed, after serving 16 years in prison for a crime that they did not commit.

• Robert Maxwell is found dead in mysterious circumstances after vanishing from his yacht off the Canary Islands; his business empire later collapses amid allegations of fraud.

1992

• Windsor Castle goes up in flames, rounding off the Queen's *'annus horribilis'*.

1993

• The European Union comes into being with the implementation of the Maastricht Treaty.

• Princess Diana announces her retirement from public life.

1994

• The Channel Tunnel officially opens.

• £7 million is spent on the first day of Lottery sales.

1995

• Nick Leeson is arrested in Germany for causing the collapse of Barings Bank, after gambling on high-risk derivatives on the Singapore market.

• Major submits himself to leadership re-election, and wins.

• In London, sales of beef drop by 10 per cent, and prices drop by 12 per cent, following another BSE scare.

Britain's most famous retired couple: Victor and Margaret Meldrew in BBC1's *One Foot in the Grave*.

Here's an Alternative

Retirement around the World

Here in the West, our industrial society, and the way
in which we separate the working environment and
the domestic sphere, means that retirement is more
important to us than it might be to an individual in,
for example, the Amazon rainforest. Nevertheless,
many different societies celebrate what is seen as the
transition into a
new and highly
significant stage of
life; at round
about the age of
retirement, your
status changes –
and for the better.

Re-christened

**Traditionally, the Eskimos take new
names when they become older,
hoping thereby to obtain a new
lease of life.**

Although not working in the sense that we use the
word, older people in more primitive societies do
retire, in that they no longer have to participate in
what are called 'subsistence activities' – foraging,
hunting and other physical tasks. They do, however,
continue with this lifestyle whilst they are physically
able: in Israel, a *kib-
butznik* should work
for as long as she or he
can. When people do
retire, they do not cease
to participate in the
maintenance of the
community: in fact in
many societies there

**'You can't help get-
ting older, but you
don't have to get
old.'**

George Burns

exist tasks which, it is believed, only older people can do.

In such cultures, once retirement has taken place, older members are assigned tasks that merit much respect. Their status is noticeably raised, and thus the other members insist upon reverence for, and paying homage to, those who are older.

Amongst the Kung bushmen of the Kalahari desert, only older people can control the distribution of water. It is the most valuable resource of all, and hence the most valued job, simply not given to anybody younger.

60–69 year-old males walk an average of 339 km (203 miles) per year.

60–69 year-old females walk an average of 289 km (173 miles) per year.

In the Mbuti tribe of Zaire, younger adulthood is considered to be a time of great conflict and dispute: hence no young adults are given any governmental power – authority is awarded only to those no longer involved with the difficulties of survival – hunting, and so on.

In many countries, Western or otherwise, retired people contribute financially to the activities of their younger relations, in a gesture of generosity which also gives them some economic status. In Finland, for example, the wages of the young Skolt Lapps cannot cover all their most favoured activities – snowboarding, drinking, smoking and gambling – and they thus

In the Tallensi tribe, in Ghana, a man does not 'own' himself until his father dies, and may therefore be quite advanced in years before becoming truly independent.

rely on the kindness and support of their older relatives, who receive a regular pension from the government.

Unlike the Skolt Lapps, the Japanese tend to prefer a lump sum payment to a pension on retirement: the longer you have worked for a company the larger your payment will be.

The Japanese also hold older people in very high esteem: up until 1947, the *Meiji* code contained a rite of passage for 60 year-olds called *Kanreki*, marking the transition into a new stage of life. *Kanreki* was a symbol of longevity and good fortune; individuals retired into a high status, and were consequently supported by the eldest son and his family.

Like the Japanese, other cultures believe that people who are no longer involved in day-to-day survival activities are almost sacred. In deeply religious or superstitious societies, older individuals are traditionally associated with 'Spirit power': they are viewed as the only people who gain access to the secretive but immense mystical power which lies beyond death. It is for this reason that, in times past, older members of a community have tended to fill the roles of witches, seers, or shamans: not because of their abilities in

Cilla helps contestants find love later in life on *Blind Date*.

The Big Climax

The mature part of life can be referred to as the 'grand climacteric', because it has long been believed that the 63rd year is one of great significance, when important things happen.

'black magic', but because their age is seen to be the key which unlocks great wisdom and power.

The mystical element of this stage in life is also reflected, in religious terms, in Hindu culture. The earlier stage of adult life is called *grhastha*, but it is considered profane and unimportant. The following stage, however – *sannyasi* – is the most holy, deserving complete and awe-struck reverence.

It is generally agreed, then, and in most cultures, that the older you are, the more socially, mentally and superior you are – something well worth bearing in mind.

The Post-Workout

Dr David Haslam

It's arrived. Retirement is upon you, and it is likely that you will be facing the prospect with a curious mixture of anticipation, excitement, relief, and dread. After all, there can be few more profound milestones in any of our lives.

The average retirement age is now 60 years. By the time you reach this age, chances are that your children will have grown and flown; you may well have grand-children; and your role in the family and the world will have changed dramatically compared to 20 years ago, when you were a mere youngster of 40. But you know that you are not old. For almost everyone, old age is 15 years older than whatever age they are now; and these days, many people of retirement age are far more active than their predecessors of earlier gener-ations.

In the past, retirement was seen in an entirely negative light. It was what you did when you no longer went out to work. Now, mercifully, all that has changed. For many people, retirement will occupy a third of their entire lifetimes. It can be a time for real enjoy-ment, activity, achievement, and fun. But this won't come automatically.

Your Changing Body
- There are obviously tremendous differences between individual retired people of the same age. Some seem active and dynamic, whilst others seem to be deteriorating rapidly. Whilst some of this is

Travelscene focussing on the over-sixties with their (then unusual) offer of holidays for older people, in 1977.

down to genetics, there is plenty of evidence that people who have a sedentary lifestyle and who smoke and drink too much will age much quicker than those who look after themselves, eat well, and stay active. Remember, it is never too late to stop smoking.

- Exercise is vital. Whilst many conditions, such as reduced muscular strength and mobility, are blamed on increasing age, they are often caused more by inactivity than by ageing itself. Regular exercise really does help to maintain your health, but if you are starting on a new exercise regime take it gently to begin with, and discuss it with your doctor first, particularly if you are currently being treated for any medical condition.

- As you get older, your metabolic rate will fall by about a fifth. So continue to enjoy a healthy, mixed diet – having good smaller meals. Unfortunately, the safe limits of alcohol are slightly lower for older people. Try to keep to an average of no more than two units a day for men, and one–two units for women.

- Sex is much too important, and fun, to be left to the young. Many couples enjoy an active sex life well into their eighties. If sex is causing you problems – either through discomfort, or an inability to 'perform' – then do discuss this with your GP. Also, men who develop problems passing urine should have their prostate gland checked.

- Recent research has confirmed something we all

know – that time really does seem to pass more quickly when you are older. Whilst toddlers have to endure an eternity between birthdays, reduced levels of a chemical called dopamine in the brains of older people fundamentally alters their perception of time. But don't forget, it only *seems* to pass more quickly. There still are 365 days in every year – even if it doesn't feel like it.

Your Changing Emotions

The age that you feel is not a constant number. There will be days when you still feel 20, and can't understand just who this person is looking back at you in the mirror. And there will be days when you feel much older – when not only do the policemen look young, but even the Pope looks young. This inconsistency of feeling can be puzzling, but it is normal.

What matters most is your attitude. If you believe that you are 'past it', then you will probably be perceived that way, too. Our peace of mind largely depends on being able to live in the present, so don't spend all your time looking back, but live for now.

It may be a cliché, but it's true: you can't take it with you. Many retired people feel obliged to save, either for the proverbial rainy day, or for their children. Your children ought to get more pleasure from you having fun now, than they would from being left money later – money whose value inflation will inevitably dilute. So spend their inheritance! After all, when are you going to do those things you always wanted to do? Now – or in the next life?

Use it or lose it. The mind and brain need to be kept active, or they will almost inevitably deteriorate. There is nothing to stop you taking up new interests, studying, learning a new language, or whatever takes your fancy. Indeed, this is the perfect time to do it.

Many people feel at a loose end when they retire, particularly if their job was one they enjoyed or found interesting. Throughout your working life, almost everyone you met will have asked, 'What do you do?' In the West, our worth in society is often measured by work: but once you retire, all that changes. Now you can be yourself, not just someone who does a job.

Indeed, if you plan your retirement wisely you will be one of those many happy people who becomes completely puzzled as to how there was ever time for work. A positive attitude is all-important. Do the things you have always wanted to do, but haven't, until now, had the time. Learn something new; take on voluntary work. Many retired people have also become fascinated by new developments such as the astonishing world of the internet.

Finally, avoid saying, 'I can't do that. I'm too old.' An attitude like that is a recipe for stagnation. You're not too old. Instead, you are now liberated from work, and probably have a third of your life left to live. Just think what previous generations would have given for that degree of luxury, and make the most of it.

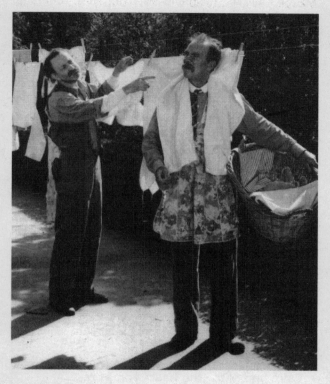

Retirement will give you the opportunity to do all those
things you've always wanted!

be 777. Noah in turn was 500 when his sons Shem, Ham and Japeth were born. Quite soon after that the troubles began. People were living just too long. Shortly before the Flood, God decreed 120 years to be the span of a man's life. Noah, however, still lived to be 950.

Methuselah, the 'man of the javelin' and son of Enoch, outlasted them all to be the oldest man in the Bible, and a symbol of longevity. At 187 he had a son, Lamech, who in turn was the father of Noah. Methuselah, incidentally, was the great-great-great-great-great-grandson of Adam, and the 11 x great-grandfather of Abraham. He lived to be 969.

'Between thirty and forty,
    one is distracted by the Five Lusts;
Between seventy and eighty,
    one is prey to a hundred diseases.
But from fifty to sixty one is free from
    all ills;
Calm and still – the heart enjoys rest...'
                              Po Chü (727–846 AD)

Copyright Notices